*To my husband H. Colin Watts,
you were my Godsent muse without knowing it.*

*To my brown girls Isabella and Laila Watts
and my brown boy Colin James Watts.*

I love you guys to the moon and back.

You can do all things through Christ.

DOING

Wattsnatural:

LIFE IN
WORDS

Latoya A. Watts

Visit our website at **www.StillwaterPress.com** for more information.

First Stillwater River Publications Edition

Library of Congress Control Number: 2020900510

ISBN: 978-1-950339-89-1

1 2 3 4 5 6 7 8 9 10
Written by Latoya A. Watts
Cover design by Emma St. Jean
Published by Stillwater River Publications, Pawtucket, RI, USA.

The views and opinions expressed in this book are solely those of the author and do not necessarily reflect the views and opinions of the publisher.

Contents

Preface

Drowning in the sea of life! But, words are my lifeline; they buoy me into a haven. It has always been my dream to write a book. Words have always been an outlet charged with electricity that gives way to wisdom and insight. In words are "the power of life and death." Where are my words birthed? In my mind and life experiences; within the joys, hurts, pains, victories, and triumphs of existence. I write from the perspective of a (P.K.) pastor's kid, from the perspective of a Black-Caribbean woman living in America. I write from the vantage point of wife, mother, educator in a form of prose meets poetry meets spoken word.

Far too long I found it easiest to write when things were at their toughest; when my emotions were at their pressure cooker max. However, recently (2018), I pledged to also write about my successes with verve. Being intentional to "shame the devil" for wanting to take those moments from me and also from my readers.

I hope the pieces of my life are an inspiration, a testament, and a guide. An art that is beautiful and open for interpretation.

LIFE

Life in words

Life has a way of bringing us together
Two loves, me and you.
I can't think of a time when I've needed you and
    you've failed.
It may have started with my go to,
"Oh, I don't know"
But, given time, we always find each other
You and me.

You give my feelings an escape
You give my thoughts a haven
And in you I find myself.

When I'm confused, you bring clarity.
And when I am angered, you provide release.
Exactly what I need, when I need it.

In you I find me.

Angels and Demons

We walk amongst angels
People placed in our lives
To pick us up when in trying situations
We walk amongst demons
People who make us angry
And propel us to indescribable frustrations

Thank you angels in the form of people
Who at my lowest have pulled me back from the brink
        of self-harm
Who at my highest, have celebrated with me
Who at my lowest points of doubt have reassured me
Thank you demons in the form of people
Who have caused me to the find the lessons in hard places
Who have taken me through the refiner's fire
Allowing me to come out pure as gold,
Precious as diamonds

To believe there are angels without demons
would be as implausible as professing there is a sky
        without earth, or a heaven without hell.

Music

Shades of blues, greens, pinks, and oranges splash across
    the morning sky; a representation of tranquility
Warm, salty, clear blue ocean waters lave feet; the ebb
    and flow like the rhythm of a heartbeat

Thump, thump, thump
Boom, boom, boom
Chhh, chhh, chhh
Cla, cla, cla
Sounds that vibrate my body
Eyes closed I can still feel the beat radiating through me
Laaah, laaah, laaah la
Buh duh, buh duh, buh duh
I hum along
Music catapults my memory to summers spent on the
    beach of King's Bay, Tobago
To long rides on the 28 bus from Mattapan to Dudley
To celebration—prom, wedding, birthdays
To "I'm in a funk, leave me alone"
The rhythms, lyrics, melodies, tempos, all mixed together
    create a puzzle that resembles a collaged canvas that
    is my life.

Rekindled

I am trying to rekindle this passion
Like long lost loves that have been out of each other's
      grasps for far too long.

The urgency to let you know and
Give room to these feelings
Is similar to a drowning swimmer's need for air

In need of an uninterrupted space, place, moment
To let it all go
Let it all out
Make room for life.
Sometimes the words are stuck,
Caught in the same way an object is caught in a
      clogged vessel.

But soon,

Like those lovers,

That swimmer,

That clogged vessel,

The words find their embrace

Receive air

And ESCAPE

To a space, place, and moment

In which to be heard.

Wattsnatural

Increased heart rate
Legs shaking
Palpitations in my chest
Feels like fingers squeezing, contracting
Like a sponge being rung and all remaining liquid expelled.

That is how I feel when I cannot speak
That is how I feel when I cannot trust
That is how I feel when you let another in

On the downswing I don't want to get out of bed
On the upswing I was to demolish, eradicate, wreck
     everything in my path.

Typhoon
Rollercoaster
Monsoon
An avalanche
Of emotions are unexplainable by unvoiced words
And so I take my pen to paper, my fingers to type.
I let my words in print express my inner most thoughts.

It is how I imagine an exonerated person must feel:
    Elated, terrified, and vulnerable
It is how I imagine being in love must feel:
Unique, accepted, peaceful, and secure
These inked thoughts are me doingwattsnatural

Climate

Memories of love filled summers
Heat from tropical sun
Cool ocean waters
Memories that prompt songs like

♪ Memories don't live like people do/ they always
    remember you ♪

                &

♪ I've had the time of my life/ I've never felt like
    this before ♪
Warm summer nights of
Youthful adventures
Walks and conversations as the sand and ocean meet
Caressing our feet
The beauty of God's creation on full display
Sunset kissed skies and
The climate of love is always a possibility
#sweetsweettnt

Without Fail

I come back to you
Time after time
Like waves crashing onto the shore.
Without fail.

I come back to you
Time after time
Like the sun in the morning sky.
Without fail.

I come back to you
Time after time
Like the moon in the night sky.
Without fail.

One day
I will not come back
Like a clock
Whose batteries have run out.

Meander

Open fields in my mind
Paths trotted
I stroll along waiting, lingering, hoping faithfully for
    your engagement

Twists, curves, shattered existence
Where do we go?
Where does this lead?
In the interim I persevere, I mature.

Meandering through this thing called life and love
Turned upside down and flipped inside out.
Heart surgically modified
By actions, thoughts, feelings

Does meandering have a destination?
When will truth eclipse hurt and pain and struggle?
Maybe when there is no longer room for growth?
Maybe when hope fades, faith is repudiated, and
I no longer exist.

Time

"You've got lots of time"
But I don't want time that adds
more months to my years, or
weeks to my months,
days to my weeks, or
hours to my days
minutes to my hours,
or seconds to my minutes

I want time that sits still
Time that envelopes me with nothingness
Time that allows me to bask in the sun, feel its warmth
    against my skin, enriching my melanin.
I want time that enables me to rest my feet in warm salty
    water as the waves approach the shore.
I want time that encapsulates moments making my
    children smile and laugh bellyful laughter sending
    stiches in their sides.
So if your "you've got time" refers to added months,
    weeks, days, hours, minutes, and seconds to do
    more endless, tedious, digging of a grave I may
    someday lay in,
you can keep your time.

In flight

Flying through clouds in the midst of turbulence,
I am still able to catch glimpses of earth below
And as I descend towards my destination
There comes a shake, a gut-wrenching startle that
      reminds me this may not be smooth travels

Despite the rough patch, I surpass.
Like a fast-moving storm,
I travail through the bumps
The end becomes clearer and more details are revealed.
What were masses in the distance now take on
      definitive shape.
Blurred images are made crystal clear

Finally, I land knowing that my purpose and mission
      have made it through their testing
I find my footing
I trod along with
my head held high
and my stride firm

Up In the Air

Let me float around up here
Unchained and free

Let me hover about
Basking in all of this beautiful creation of luscious green
      landscapes that curve and rise like a woman's physique
And feel the breeze that emit from vast oceans,
Its waves a mixture of dark blue hues bellowing of the
      lives captured by its roar
Or tropical clear greens that exude pleasure of love
      and adventure

Let me stay here
Flying through clouds that blanket me in this journey
      called life
Let me reside in the air up here where gravity cannot
      tug at me
Returning me to a reality filled with pain and disquietude

Slow Down

In the business of life,
Laser focused on all that needs to be accomplished,
I am head down,
Fast paced
Through the airport

Confronted by a stranger,
In our encounter he urges me to
Slow down,
Wander through life and enjoy the moments

"I am tired" he says
"Not of living
But of the demands of life"

Slow down,
Meander
Walk leisurely
Enjoy that cup of tea
Sip slowly
Savor the flavors
Peppermint and lemon grass
Careful of potential burns in the haste

At the next checkpoint
Leniency is not afforded
At the next checkpoint there are stipulations
Hard and fast
A stripping away to examine all possessions

Only the invaluable matter.
The moments I paused long enough
Allowing the sun to caress my melanin infused skin
Nights spent gazing at the ripples of water on the bay
Kisses planted on loved ones
And embraces which symbolize safety

At that final checkpoint
I cherish the weightless
That has kept me grounded

Massage

Hands are kneading into flesh
Pausing to apply extra pressure on areas knotted, kinked,
    and sore
Similar to my need to fix things, fix you, fix us.

Broad strokes pose an initial threat to discovery
Eventually fingers, palms, and knuckles
Expose deep and hidden places where aches reside

Pressure in those kneading moments ache,
Comparable to feet run ragged in marathons without
    training
Often I've let my emotions convey meaning
When in reality I should have let silence and joy speak
Knowing the inner working will later bring
    insurmountable relief.

Waiting

Is tough
like overcooked meat
and leather shoes
Painful like an excruciating toothache
that won't subside
Surgery without anesthesia
Sour like lemon to taste buds
after having sweet delicacies
Refining happens in the waiting

What I Suppose a Hurting Man Would Say

Can you focus on the positives for once?
Focus on the fact that I made it home last night
Focus on the fact that I'm sober today
Focus on the fact that I am living and breathing

Can you focus on my ability to provide and be present?
Focus on the fact that that once upon a time distraction
    no longer holds my attention

Can you acknowledge my presence in the house of
    the Lord?
Acknowledge my outstretched arms and head nods
    as surrender
Appreciate my time spent with the kids
Appreciate my support of your parenting styles

Can you appreciate my growth and development as a man?
My fragile state as I strive to be a *better* man
Respect my strides towards being a man after God's
      own heart

Just watch me

Also the things I suppose a healing man would say

Grave Indifference

Do you see me?
Can you hear me?
Open your eyes
Open your ears
See…listen
Not just with physical orifices
But with your heart.

Lives lost
Lives wasted
Lives that ooze like puss infected
wounds waiting to be cut open
and drained

How then will these noxious
thoughts, habits, and behaviors
Be woven?
Will they or have they already become a complacent part
   of our society?

The hatred
The lack of sentiment

Do you hear our young people who scream hashtags
#nomore
#metoo
#blacklivesmatter
Do you see our young people declaring
MY LIFE MATTERS?

Do you see
Our students, marginalized by a system
set up to fail them?
Do you hear
Their pleas, evident by
Social services
Truancy
Court hearings
And loss?

Or, have you shown grave indifference…?
Such an oxymoron!

Next to Last Mistake

Imperfect like
Young fruit forced to ripen
Young lady, a mother before her time
Young boy, imprisoned, before he is even a man
Mistake.

Life annihilated
Due to unjust laws and systems
Birth aborted
Initiated by decisions beyond control

Another mistake
Next to last mistake,
Is there such a thing?
Can mistakes be predicted?
Prevented?
Or are mistakes simply lessons yet to be learned?

Status of Dreams

Deferred like Frost
For equality like King
Interpreted by Joseph
Hold fast says Hughes
An act for immigrants
What is the status of your dreams?

Roots

You see my brokenness yet you love me
You see my faults yet you look at me as though I am
      perfection

Like roots that grow deeper
that is the description of my love for you.
Over time those roots begin to form and
new buds emerge, revealing signs of life
In time fresh roots are transplanted
adapting to a new home in soil that will nurture growth.

As those roots grow, new buds transform
Similarly my love for you swells like pregnancy.
Roots will eventually outgrow, become claustrophobic,
      and stagnate in their current environment

I desire for us to be transplanted
Where we grow, learn, support, and evolve
Eventually needing a new space
that can contain for another season roots that will
     again extend

As roots develop, they germinate stems and buds
Creating replicas, yet
given the freedom to be their own.

Share Black Man

Dear Black man,
I see the weights you carry
Both visible and invisible
I see your desire to cocoon your emotions
I know of your reticence.
Guess what Black man?
It's time to share Black man.

Share the nightmares that jolt you awake at night
Share the hurts you've refused to divulge for years
Share them with your therapist
Yes I said therapist
Because yes Black man
It's okay to have one of those.
Share with your significant other,
The instinct to help in any way possible
Is symbolic of their love for you.

Whatever you do Black man,
It's time to put in the work
To get rid of those walls
It's okay to let people in
It's okay to relinquish the weights, offenses, and baggage
Share joy, share stories of boisterous experiences that
      have kept you going
It's time Black man
It's time to share.

Alone

Friends,
Who needs them?
We all do.
But there is something to be said for alone time.
No kids,
No spouse,
No family,
No friends vying for attention, guidance, and love.
There is something to be said for alone time
Time with thoughts
Time to catch a game
Time to soak in the tub
Time to love on oneself
Simply alone

FAITH

Prayers (i)

Of a grandmother
Of a mother
Of a wife
Of a friend
Of a confidant

Prayers for generational blessings
Prayers for togetherness
Prayers for purpose
Prayers for deliverance
Prayers for peace

Sent to the throne of heaven
On our behalf
Sometimes unbeknownst to us
To a God that hears them all
And answers in perfect time

Being Saved

Unfiltered
Wretched
Undignified mess

Being saved
And Spirit filled
Guides me into all truth
If I were not,
Hot dang!
I'd be that mess!

Thoughts of drinks that numb shame are alleviated
through my Praise
Thoughts of hurt and pain are released by my prayers
Dark clouds and feelings of self-harm are engulfed by
the reminder of His love.
He is:
A friend.
A savior with
A love
So deep.
Nonjudgmental, always forgiving, always present.
Always perfect in my weakness.
I will run to You my savior
Every time.

I am Not a Savior

I pray for you
I cry for you
I give for you
But I am NOT a savior
                I have realized that now

I encourage
I support
The best way I know how
Even in silence
But I am NOT a savior
                    I know that now

I continue to pray
I continue to support
And at times I know I will cry
From lack of understanding
Knowing that
                    I am NOT a savior

There is however, one true savior
He died for you and me
Performed endless miracles
And called us onto himself
He holds it ALL, can give it ALL
He is the Savior

Jesus Christ, Elohim.

On my Knees, at the Feet of Jesus

You keep me at the feet of Jesus
I credit you that.
You keep me at the feet of Jesus
When I am insecure and doubtful of your actions
When I see where our children need guidance, direction,
        and hands on prayer that you infrequently provide

You keep me at the feet of Jesus
When I see the potential and calling on your life
That you don't always live up to

You keep me at the feet of Jesus
And I credit you that
Because It is at the feet of Jesus that I am
Rejuvenated and encouraged
Affirmed and loved,
Experiencing my breakthrough.

Holy Spirit

Countless times I've thought about
"Giving you a piece of my mind"
"Flying off the handle"
"Cussin' you out"
Then indescribable quiet washes over me and steals the
      words and
BLOCKS the flow of easy release
A quiet that I can only credit as the Holy Spirit

At times when I want to ensure my opinion is heard and
      understood no matter the cost
I am often jolted mute
Silenced into thoughts of what is best in the end
"Blessed are the peacemakers"
"Slow to speak, slow to anger"
All reminders of that sweet Holy Spirit

Elixir

Sweet syrupy substance oozes its way
Down my throat
Tart, harsh, brolic, acidic
Numbing my senses
Annihilating my sensibility

Annihilating my sensibility
That I cannot differentiate
Truth from lie
Love from hate
Pain from joy

Love from hate
Evil as the serpent who lured Eve into
Denial of who she was destined to be
Rescinding her God given position as ideal
Wife and lover; bone of his bone, flesh of his flesh

Rescinding her God given position as ideal
She drinks in elixir that
Medicates the hurt and transports her to a
Place of perceived comfort
Only to be convicted and conflicted

Place of perceived comfort
I get comfortable as this sweet substance
Moves through me causing me to lose myself
Become myself in a completely different manner
Dabbling in treacherous and uncharted situations

Becoming myself in a completely different manner
I lose sight of my calling with every sip,
Every ounce, every pint, every gallon
Only to face the demons that are chasing me
Once that sweet elixir leaves my body

Only to face the demons that are chasing me:
You aren't good enough
You aren't worth the time
You are a product of brokenness
But wait!

You are a product of brokenness
His broken body for your transgressions
His broken body as a symbol of His love for you
His broken body for your life, my life
Brining life and light

His Spirit becomes a replacement for elixir
That can too easily blind true vision of a called purpose
A called destiny
A true self.

Revelation

Life and death are in the power of the tongue
This I know as truth
Yet I speak recklessly
My thoughts are foul
And I have selfish ambitions

It was that day
The day of revelation,
I realized I had spoken the wrong words
and prayed the wrong prayers.
What I needed to pray for was your salvation.

My Take on Faith

I was "born and raised" in church. For years and years all I knew was home, school, church. When I was old enough, it was home, school, church, work, and repeat. As a pastor's kid, church wasn't an option as long as I lived under my parents' roof. It. Was. Mandatory.

Then I found love, college rolled around, and in those formidable experiences and years I encountered God for myself. I understood what sowing a hundred-dollar seed from my minimum wage job would do... open the door to a full college scholarship. I discovered what the break-up of an "unequally yoked" relationship would bring... a divine union with purpose. I was able to comprehend what being in a car wreck at six months pregnant and walking away unscathed means... heavenly protection with the intent of living out purpose.

For me, Faith=Purpose=An intimate relationship with God. None of this is to say there weren't moments I did not question God. Trust me, I definitely had those moments! I questioned God when my parents (pastors) couldn't find a way to reconcile their marriage. I questioned God when living paycheck to paycheck, despite paying tithes, was my reality. I questioned God when the unexpected death of a loved one hit close to home. The most trying for me personally? I question God when my marriage goes through rocky and seemingly irreconcilable seasons.

Nonetheless, the goodness of God has far outweighed my questions. He has showed up for me time after time. In my moments of dark despair He rescued me. In all my doubt I choose to believe there is a God. Because, like the recording artist Lecrae says, "If I'm wrong about God then I've wasted my life. If you're wrong about God then you've wasted your eternity." I chose to believe and live my life accordingly. No regrets!

IDENTITY

unfinished

marked and labeled

titles that outwardly and inwardly depict who I am

i have accepted the labels as part of my identity:

daughter

wife

mother

pastor's kid

middle child

introvert

Shambles

I am broken,

Shattered glass on a tiled floor

I am torn

Tattered rags strewn about

I am lost

Bewildered by thoughts unimaginable

I am

    Grieving

    Strong

    Emotionless

    Hopeful

I know the theoretical outcome

However, the practical reality of now is difficult.

But God… I trust You

Out on a Limb

Introvert
Socially awkward
I sit and fidget with anything that makes me blend into
     the background
Camouflaged by all that is taking place around me

I don't belong here
Or do I?
For that matter, do I belong anywhere?
Floating through life
Waiting for a sense of belonging

At age 12
I glared in the mirror
despising the person looking back at me
Pills in hand
thinking what's the use?
Out on a limb not wanting a lifeline

Twenty years later I walk past that same reflection and think
God I thank You for allowing me to see my beauty and
my worth
At 13
I couldn't recognize it
At 15
I didn't value it
At 16
I let others take advantage of it
At 19
I settled for less
And at 21
I became privy to the certainty that I was not created
to please man;
I was created to live out my purpose.

2 truths and a lie

I know who I am
I am daughter of the most High King
Every microgram
Of being, specially crafted to His liking
I know who I am
I am granddaughter of a super matriarch
Visual phonocardiogram
Of a legend who's physical body departed in March

I embrace unwavering truth,
Of professed love
Trusting like a child
The fairytales of love
Heart beating, heart longing, never negated
Releasing all doubt like a dove

Little loves have etched
Their mark on my life
Like strings that maneuver a puppet, attached
They give me life, life, life

Shell

You have your way with my body
But there is no emotional connection
I am a shell
You feed me words
That I no longer believe
Words I once cherished,
However,
I am now a shell
Is there any substance within this shell?
Will it one day break to reveal its true essence
Like that of an oyster?
Or will the broken unattractive, outward shell
Define the beauty hidden within?

Size

Yuh throw off size   Yuh puh on size

Yuh starting to

rung off

Gyal like life

treatin'

yuh good

Marrid life going   well fuh yuh

Weh yuh going   wid all dah size?

Dah size nah

'gree wid yuh

body shaming phrases from my Caribbean peoples

Spring Training

Dysmorphia.
I look into the mirror and
See the shades
Of skin that differ around my belly button
Revealing stretch marks
That mark the process and phases of carrying life within me.

Dysmorphia.
I look in the mirror and think "will he find another
because my stomach isn't flat
and my breasts sag from having nursed three beautiful
    babies?"
Dysmorphia
Of the brain
Because I see those marks as significant as the umbilical
    cords that connected my life
To their lives,
To their heart beats,
That lived within me.
Those marks have taken up permanent residence
    on my flesh.
Yet my brain asks
Beauty or flaws?

Spring brings forth newness like flowers peeking out
    of dirt.
Embracing new life and the beauty they will soon reveal.

Training my brain to love every inch of who I am.
From the kink of my unruly curls
To the imperfectly perfect folds of skin and
    multicolored marks.

Training my brain to accept the beauty that
has risen out of dirt, covered in earth (trampled on)
Covered in scars (emotionally, mentally, and physically)

Dysmorphia I expel you.
Like Spring training,
Newness has arrived!

Evolution

I am constantly evolving, learning maturing, and
    morphing into a newer, better, more beautiful me.
From caterpillar to butterfly
Ecdysis, The process of a snake shedding its skin
Shedding skin to rid itself of parasites.
To allow for further growth,
I too shed the parasites of
Lies
Mistrust
Un-forgiveness
Doubt
AND
Caring
Too
Damn
Much
About what others have to say

Profile

Sometimes I look in the mirror and think
girl you so flyyy
Head wrapped
High, curly, ponytail
Skin free of makeup
In all my natural, God given splendor

However, I get caught by an audacious retort and
Almost buy the lie
The devil tried to feed me
That my nose is too broad
And my side profile does not fit *the* profile.

Just as quickly
I am reminded that my outward profile
Is not always a reflection of my inward beauty
Which permeates:
Patience
Love
Sacrifice
Forgiveness.
I am beauty personified

Opinion

Your opinion of me
Does not define my beauty
I am whole
I haven't always been this way
Nevertheless, here I am
At peace with myself
At peace with my body
At peace with my thoughts

Your opinion of me
Will no longer belittle my worth
I haven't always believed these truths
Nevertheless, here I am
At peace with my dreams
At peace with releasing my past
At peace with what the future may bring

The only opinions that matter

Are those I choose to believe

The ones my creator deemed fit for my description:

- ✓ Fearfully and wonderfully made
- ✓ Loved
- ✓ Good
- ✓ Blessed
- ✓ Favored
- ✓ A new creation with old things gone

Your opinion no longer enslaves me

P.K. (Pastor's Kid)

Ooo, you're a pastor's kid?
I've heard that question too numerous of times to track
As though to really ask:
You must be saved, sanctified, and Holy Ghost filled?
Or the contrary:
And you act like that?

Yep, that's Pastor Ray and Sis. Joy's children
Born in the church,
Rooted in a foundation of
Proverbs induced Saturdays
Family devotions
Church meetings
Speaking in tongues
Sword drills
VBS
Prayer and Fasts

Contrasted with
Hurt
Adultery
Lies
Complacency

Unpruned branches
Non negotiables

Living in moments of seized breath whenever groups of
        pastors are assembled
Fear of what may escape the lips that once preached the
        gospel, now living an estranged life
A life of pointed fingers casting blame
A life of pride, too pompous to make amends
And hearts too calloused to forgive.
What happened to those preached words?
What happened to those truths?
Were they ever truths you believed yourself?

Pastor's kids,
Left to face the trials while standing on a foundation
        shaken
A foundation I must recreate and solidify as my own
A foundation I pray will now withstand the thunderous
        blasts of life.

Other

- ☐ ~~Black~~
- ☐ ~~White/Caucasian~~
- ☐ ~~Hispanic~~
- ☑ Other

I chose other because Black, although apparently so from
    first glance, does not define the entirety of who I am
Selecting Black, boxes me in

My childhood upbringing did not lend to a relational or
    empathetic consciousness of the Black American
    experience.
If simply comparing my complexion to that of colors
    stacked in a box of 23 other shades I am not black
    but in fact a shade of cacao beans, like those my
    grandmother fleshed from fresh yellow fruit set out
    to dry.

Black does not encapsulate that my
Maternal great-grandmother was the product of a
    Scottish plantation owner.
Colonizer of my island Tobago
A mystery still, whether that procreation was true love
    or possession.

Black does not encapsulate that my
Paternal great-grandfather was the product of Chinese
    natives in Guyana
Whether true natives or colonizers, the debate still ongoing.

Black does not encapsulate that my maternal grandfather
    was the direct offspring of slaves in the Caribbean
With roots so bound to the motherland, that stories of
    Spirits and witchcraft physically propelling them
    across oceans are a part of my family history.

Being Black
Means I am product of the motherland
Product of freed people
Forced to be
OTHER

Being Black
Means I am product of
Colonizers in foreign lands dominating people and
property not theirs, making them
OTHER

Being Black
Means appreciating my
African, Scottish, Chinese Caribbean, South American
self as
OTHER

Fed Race

People talk about race consciousness
I was ignorant until I left my little island of Tobago and
    ventured into the great land of opportunity my
    parents spoke about.

They were fed the dream of opportunities from their
    older siblings who tarried in the chartered waters
    before them.
They were fed the American Dream
Similar to the Egyptian's trek to Canaan
A land that flowed of milk and honey
The promise land my parents read about and taught
    as pastors.

On my little island I was sheltered from any real plight
    of race and the cruelties inflicted by one human to
    another even though I read of such atrocities in the
    very Bible I was spoon fed.
I was shielded from the injustices I would eventually
    encounter.

On my little island issues of race was between the Indian
    man and the black man
The oppressions more about class,
The struggle more about colorism, mannerisms,
    and religion.

On my island I was a gem, covered by earth not yet
    exposed
And for years after migrating to the U.S., I lived in
    naiveté; until curiosity met love.
My bible basics were questioned
My race blindness evoked with stories others had endured.
Until that point, in my mind, we were all simply God's
    children. I knew no difference, saw no difference.

I was removed from my island
Like the people of Israel questioning their removal from
     Egypt. In a quest through desolate lands
No resemblance of a promise.
In America love showed me centuries of hardship and
     injustices live by the Black race
In America love sparked my inquisitiveness
Time and time again when confronted by harsh realities
     I desire to know love's perspective

I transitioned from my little island of Tobago, where
     everything was seemingly innocuous, only to
     witness God's creation as marginalized and
     subhuman in a vast land where I was fed race

A Briefing on my Identity Journey

My default is to see the good in people. (That is, unless you've done me wrong. Bear with me, God ain't through with me yet.) Call it naïve. Call it living in a bubble. Call it sheltered. Call me a "gem"—my favorite compliment by far, which could have been taken as an insult. As if to say you are covered, ignorant, reside in dirt. But I defaulted to the good. What resonated with me was that you are treasured, protected, and radiant once unearthed.

I grasped that my default was an easy out for a lot of people I encountered and interacted with. Having conversations over the years has allowed me to see the credence of people's true nature and take hold of my own reality. I had unconsciously allowed people to perpetuate their prejudices, stereotypes, racism, and bigotry. For example:

Prior to my migration to the U.S., I never thought twice about my name. In elementary school where people called me Latoya Jackson, it clicked that my name had more associated with it than this small island girl born to Christian parents thought. As I approached employment age, I heard numerous stories of individuals' inability to get a job due to their names. Seemingly ethnic or difficult to pronounce names were shuffled to the bottom of hiring piles. I was convinced that once I turned eighteen, I would legally change my name because, let's be honest, how many white Latoyas do you know? (I have since run into such person.) That sigma weighed heavily on me as I chose names for my own children. I was determined to give them names that wouldn't place them at a disadvantage without first getting to know them. Finally, as a woman in my mid-thirties, I am thankfully able to embrace that my name is identifiably woman of color. No more hiding.

Another post migration story: I had developed deep visceral feelings about Jamaicans, and harboured them for quite some time. During elementary and middle school with heavy accent in tow, it seemed that Jamaica was the only Caribbean accent and country known to man. This infuriated me. No, people! There are other Caribbean countries out there—a sentiment I am sure other cultural groups can attest to. In addition, as much as I hate to admit, people's comments heavily impacted how I self-identified. Being told "you have nice hair for a black girl" and being asked to speak on a subject because I was the only Christian or person of color in a room, as though my opinion was the only one that carried weight, posed challenges of their own. I have been gawked at and bombarded with questions for having my hair wrapped (pre-natural stage) and had twists pulled (mid natural phase) by grown people, none of which ever fazed me. My thought: they don't know any better. In reality, I was enabling.

I have accepted that my default is not a handicap but rather a strength. However, my choosing to see the good in people now comes with the ability to call individuals out on their lack of owning their shortcomings and ignorance. I am not free to speak my truth.

LOVE & MARRIAGE

Back Pocket

Convenient safety net
I reach for you, into you
Whenever I choose.
You have the ability to comfort me

Your secured placement
Allows me to extract from you
The memories that were once at
The forefront of my mind
Now suppressed with elapsed time

Ahh… I can reach for you
When low, lonely, wishful, doubtful,
In need of a pick me up
There you are
Ready with open space
Inviting care
You are my back my pocket babe

Young Love

Moments when young explorative and inquisitive souls
        seek clarity I think of you
I think of moments where my youthful self desired to
        always be in your company
I reminisce about ways in which just knowing you
        allowed me to find myself
You pushed me to be a better me and I hope I did the
        same for you
We laughed
We competed
We loved
We defied the odds
Then it came crashing to a halt!
Brakes mashed hard in anticipation of a head on collision

Unequally yoked they said

Not going to work they said

Yet I fought to keep you close

Fought to hold on to our piece of heaven here on earth

Memories, love notes, all material symbols of a love that
could never be

Dreams dashed,

Scattered like fall leaves in a whirling breeze.

In youth we lived; in youth our love ended.

A Note to my Husband

Time. They say time heals all wounds. And
Age. With age comes wisdom.

I thank God for both time and age.
For with time and age I have grown to love you.

More than the day we met
Differently than the day we married
Deeper than our intimate encounters.

I love you more than the butterflies that filled my
    stomach during courtship
I love you with a different light than that which
    illuminated the room the evening we said "I do"
I love you deeper than the thrusts of your love as it meets
    my passion
I love our evolution
I love you.

Muse

You inspire me.
When I think of love I think of you
I think of long bus rides,
Stolen moments,
Giggles, and a stomach churning with butterflies.

When I think of love I think of you.
I think of hurt
I think of possibilities never materialized
Of dreams forgotten once awake,
Of words,
On paper drenched in water
Faded with no chance of recovery

Nonetheless, you inspire me
To express myself
Despite the turmoil
Despite the doubt,
Despite the sorrow,
To love without fail
To love beyond myself
To be me

Portrait of My Husband

Chocolate brown
Tall and handsome as your mind's eye will allow you
    to create
6'0, lean and a signature stroll

Black hair, cropped low, with early grays sprinkled
    in-between
Thick eyebrows introduce eyes that conceal thoughts and
    emotions unshared
Broad nose and
A moustache that frames full lips that beckon me to
    kiss them,
I draw them in, nibble gently, yet, with intense craving.

Slender shoulders, but strong enough to carry the weight
    of our family
Arms long, that when held in an embrace transcend
    warmth imaginable
Long torso, long legs
Supported by a booty shaped like rain drops. Shaped like
    perfection.

Feet wide, feet flat.
Feet that I pray will lead and walk the path destined by
    our heavenly Father.

The portrait of a man created by God
Has an insatiable personality
That makes you happy and mad simultaneously
A man hurting, questioning, searching
To find an inner peace that can only come from God

A man I declare to be bold like John, steadfast like Paul,
    faithful like Abraham, humble like Moses, and full
    of pursuit like David,

All in his own right

Embrace

I find warmth in your embrace
Long, extended embraces that make
the feelings of anger dissolve and vanish.
Embraces that extinguish doubt, hurt, and shame

Embraces engulf me like clouds
cushioning skies on an overcast day.
Embraces draw me in like an artists' charcoal on canvas
That tells a story only the two can truly understand.

Beyond Question

"Do you love me?" he asks
Beyond question
"How much do you love me?"
As deep as the ocean
As long as the Nile
So much that forgiveness is granted over and over and
over again
"Do I love you?"
I respond:
Beyond question

Trapped

Trapped

Caught

Bound like morsels trying to escape a sieve

Tears will not come

They have calloused like unworked, untrained, virgin
> fingers learning to play a guitar

They are obstructed like boulders blocking and diverting
> the flow of water down a stream

They long for an escape but are

Trapped

Caught and

Bound

They are hostage to this thing called love

A Love Like Ours (i)

Loud voices
Harsh tones
Disagreements
Points of views
Expressed feelings
Understanding
Reconciliation and growth
A lot of God's grace
Maintaining a love like ours

Sleepless

Thoughts of you
Thoughts of us
Flood through my mind
I want to love you with every core of my being
But being hurt over and over again by thoughtless
Actions restrict and bind my ability to carry out that
    boundless love.

Is it possible for one to love unconditionally
If not for God himself?
Is it possible to give selflessly
If not for God himself?

I realize that the more I love God,
The more I am able to love you.
His agape love for me,
Streams over to love I can so freely give you

Forever Love

I drive by couples in long embraces
And remember days of
Affection
Sweet caresses
And my mama's observation of a smile so bright she'd ask,
"Who's been whispering sweet nothings in your ear?"
I smile at those couples that appear to have never been
      tainted by hurt.
They embrace the bliss of a love bound to last.
As time pauses for them,
In moments of embraces
In moments together
Their forever love is encapsulated.

Climactic Symphony

Your tongue
Touching my flesh
Sounds of a symphony,
A perfect harmony,
As my cries and laughter of pleasure enter the air.
Tongue touching flesh
Produce a climactic symphony

A Love Like Ours (ii)

Loud voices
Like subway musicians beating their feelings on
    plastic buckets

Harsh tones
That startle an infant,
The unexpected sound of an 18 wheeler's horn

Disagreements and opposing point of views
Plaintiff vs. Defendant
Jurors out with a verdict

Expressed feelings eventually lead to understanding
Reconciliation and growth possible with
A lot of God's grace

All of this indicative of
A love like ours

Amorous Rebuttal

Face painted, beat
Seemingly perfect features
Conceal dark thoughts of a contrived love.
Eyes wide with lust
Perceptions of what could be
She molded and crafted an augmented reality

Must have it
Must have him
She thought
Not comprehending
That concealed dark thoughts of a contrived love
Or cognizant of desires created in mind's eye
If materialized can eat away at souls

Invest more

Give more

Believe more

She convinced herself

Only to be rejected,

Dejected, ejected from a

Molded, crafted, augmented reality

Only to realize the

Game

is

Over.

Soul Ties

Soul ties
will have you tied up,
knotted and in shreds if not careful
Soul ties
Like shoelaces belonging to a child still trying to get it right
form jumbles and frays
Soul ties
Like weeds with stubborn roots tangle and make
    landscaped beauty unsightly
Soul ties
Like mishandled and unkempt yarn
have ends in sight but no clear path from one point to
    the next
Baby my soul is tied to yours
I gave you my soul
and never dreamt I'd ask for it back
However, reclaiming it
Required me to do some work
To discover myself
To untangle emotional baggage
A luxury that giving you my soul I can no longer afford
I need to be whole,
Untethered to lies and the mixture of other souls

I never gave permission to be a part of our union
I am releasing these ties
Giving them wings like once caged birds
In order for my soul to find a home
Not with clipped wings and a caged song
But with a soaring freedom

Investment

Years invested
Sacrifices made
But differences never set aside for a common goal

Lost sight of God's plan
Chose to do his own thing
Chose to neglect his calling
Chose to harden his heart
Smiles
Masked hurt, turmoil, adultery, and lies.
Somber expressions
Were Indicators for help; an appeal for a lifeline
From people deemed covering and leadership
Only to be left in solace.
Thankfully finding peace in the best place possible
God! ABBA father!

Years invested and thankfully
The mighty hand of God still covered and protected
        offspring that would one day call her blessed.
How do we call one blessed, yet curse the other?
A pair that should have lasted forever,
'til death do them part

Generations later questions that plea to know truths
    are unearthed
Questions that evoke emotions
"Where did you come from mommy?"
My response:
I am from once upon a time pastors.
I am from a broken marriage
I am from a praying grandmother, a praying mother.
Matriarchs with legacies that will last from generation
    to generation.
Questions that evoke emotions
Where are you going mommy?"
My response:
I am going up yonder
I am living with a God centered eternity in mind
I am going to show you the way and pray without
    ceasing that you my children chose to walk in the
    way that leads to Him.

Whenever I try to walk away from you

I am reminded of God,
Of His unconditional love
I am reminded of living things
If neglected, will surely die
But given love –in all manner
Will thrive again
With that I remain rooted

I Got You

I uttered those words without realizing the weight
And magnitude to which they would hold me
Pain, grief, and death has a way of impressing and
      propelling us to dark places.

Stamped with labels
Running from purpose
Running to distraction

Reflecting on "I got you"
I know that those words will keep me grounded
Those three simple words would stretch me beyond myself

Grounded to a purpose
Grounded to a calling
Grounded to be yours
Not begrudgingly
But with love and
In prayer

A shoulder to cry on
Ears that will listen
An embrace that will hold the gravity of expressed and
      suppressed grief
Through it all
"I got you"

#theevolution

Many have heard, read, or come across portions of the scripture on love at some point. "Love is patient, love is kind. It does not envy, it does not boast, it is not proud. It does not dishonor others, it is not self-seeking, it is not easily angered, it keeps no record of wrongs. Love does not delight in evil but rejoices with the truth. It always protects, always trusts, always hopes, always perseveres. Love never fails." I Corinthians 13: 4-8 (NIV).

Man have I been guilty of loving imperfectly! Failing and attempting; failing and attempting again. I guess you can say I have mastered the "love perseveres" portion of that scripture. One thing I found to be true about my ability to love: I couldn't begin to love until I accepted that God loves me. Then and only then can I love like He does. Forgiving constantly and keeping no record of wrongs. This is not an easy thing to do. Not. By. Any. Means. However, with every hurt I have experienced, be it from a loved one, a friend, or a stranger, I have learned to love beyond the capacity I thought possible.

Leading up to my 10th wedding anniversary, I compiled a list that I still refer to often.

Things I've learned and understood better over the last 10 years:

1. The phrase we all need a little dirt to grow
2. Sometimes in relationships things aren't only, or always black-and-white
3. What doesn't kill you makes you stronger or at least wiser
4. Forgiveness is more important for the one granting forgiveness than the one receiving forgiveness
5. Marriage is a covenant and commitment between two people
6. Give room for vents without judgement
7. Post vents, allow yourself and your spouse to heal
8. Love your spouse for who they are, while keeping who they could/are supposed to be in prayer
9. You both have to say divorce is not an option, and mean divorce is not an option in order for it to be true
10. Most importantly, without God and prayer we wouldn't have made it thus far.

I appreciate the lessons love and marriage has taught me over the years, and I welcome the growth yet to come.

MOTHERHOOD & FAMILY

Legacy (i)

Innocent, beautiful, pure, faultless
Little girl,
Embrace your truths

Revelations, alive, woke
Young lady,
Do not ignore or underestimate your possibilities

Wise, experienced, full of knowledge
Woman
Embody your worth

Timeless, ageless, full of wisdom
Grandmother
We acknowledge your legacy

Un...

Life
Undeveloped
Underappreciated
Unveiled
Unseen
Untold
Unconscious
Unknown
But know, you were never
Unloved

What if...

What if... It never happened? Would I be a stronger person?

What if... I said no? Followed my gut?

What if... I too died?

What if... I never get over this loss?

What if... I lose another?

What if... I stopped being selfish? Or am I?

What if... I am not allowed to grieve?

Don't walk this way

Don't walk this way my child.
The way that is filled with lies, superficial beauty, and the
     pull of society
Like the Proverb says: heed my words.

Don't walk this way my child.
The way of regrets,
It can save you a world of heartache.

Know your worth and value it.
My daughters you are loved by a man whom no earthly
     one can compare

My son, make God your compass and pilot,
That you may lead with integrity, honesty, and true poise

Listen to my words my child and
Be sure not to walk this way.
The way that causes you to lose your way
And repeat never ending cycles.
Walk the way of light and truth
Walk the way set before you by the Almighty God.
And you will win
EVERY TIME

Queen

Hold your head high
you are a princess now,
but a queen in the making
Your mind more valuable than the worth any man may
    try to put on that which lies
At the meeting of your thighs

Hold your head high
You are steward to the gifts, blessings, and knowledge
    that lie within you
Spend time in exploration and development
Mine the diamonds in the rough
For in time He will amplify

Hold your head high
you are a princess now
but a queen in the making
Hone these truths
Accept these truths
Not up for debate or any to nullify

Brown King

You think you are a
Ninja
Superman
Black Panther
Captain America
Flash

I see my brown boy
Full of love and emotions
Caring and charming

My brown boy
Do not let this world harden you where you are
  constantly fighting demons
Forming a heart of steel that even kryptonite cannot
  penetrate
Becoming a token image of a land deemed worthless
Casting shields as a means of protection
While moving fast, fast, unable to grasp that which is yours

You are free my brown boy who will grow into a
    handsome king
Capable of crying publicly
Capable of articulating your feelings
Capable of loving unapologetically
Capable of breaking stereotypes that

being born
in
the
skin
you're
in
may want to box you
in

You are capable of being an exemplary priest and king of
    your destiny

Open Letters to my Children

I love you more than words could explain! But an attempt I will make. Your first heartbeats resided within me which gave me a joy that out measures a fat kid's love for cake (or in my case ice-cream), a peanut butter and jelly connection, a salt and pepper combination and all other like euphemisms.

I see the prayers I prayed over you while yet in my womb manifest each and every day. From the seemingly meaningless things like: God please let Belle have long hair like mine with texture like her daddy's. And, may Laila always speak the truth, and God if this is a boy, may he be the one to keep his sisters in line should they ever stray away from You.

In your walk through life, I pray for you all a heartfelt prayer; that the God I serve will bestow all that you will ever need. I pray for your relationships with Him to be one of true and divine intimacy. A knowing Him for yourself.

My hopes and prayers:
1. That you all are better individuals than I have ever been, I am, or I will ever be.
2. That you find true love with Belle one man, Laila one man, and Ceej one woman. That your spouses

will love you solely, whole heartedly, without cravings, eyes, heart, or body for anyone else and vice versa.

3. That you find success in life doing that which is honest and your true life's joy.

Isabella: I pray you find freedom in who you are. You are a gentle spirit, honest, fierce in your own right and loved. Sing to the music of your heart.

Laila: you are outwardly feisty and I pray you will never let the enemy get a foothold on your life. May you ALWAYS speak the unadulterated word and truth of God. Love fairly.

My Ceejypoo: remain kind! Love one woman and one woman only. I pray she will always be your enough. I pray that God will send the right woman to support, build you up, and encourage you in life's walk always.

~*~ : You are safe in His arms. The chance I never got. I can't imagine what would have been.

My babies, you are loved. You are blessed. You are His children. You have purpose.

Acknowledgements

There are countless individuals who have aided me in the process of getting this book out of my mind and into your hands. To my husband H. Colin Watts and kiddos (Isabella, Laila, and Colin James Watts), I love, love, love you guys. You all are my motivation, the reason I keep pressing on, and the muse to this book child.

I would like to thank my sisters (Nikki and Jewel Williams) for allowing me to share my dream, ideas, and pieces of my work with them along the way –even though they didn't have much of a choice. ☺ To my mom (Jonetter Williams) thank you so much for watching the kids when I needed a space to think, write, attend a meeting, etc. and my dad (Ray Williams) for always pushing us kids to be business minded individuals.

Thank you Carrie Caoutte-de Lallo for reading my first draft, providing me with feedback, and the warm encouragement to keep writing. Desiree Gamble you are the ultimate Latoya hype woman; I appreciate you!

To my father-in-law, James A.S. Watts, thank you for speaking over me and believing I could do this even before I was your daughter-in-law. R.I.P.

I also acknowledge that without life's struggles I would not have been able to write this book. For "we can rejoice, too, when we run into problems and trials, for we know that they help us develop endurance. And endurance develops strength of character, and character strengthens our confident hope of salvation." Rom. 5:3-4 NLT.

Until next time.

JUST PLANT SEEDS

A Message of Hope for Religious Educators

JARED DEES